Buttercream Dreams

JEFF MARTIN • PHOTOGRAPHY BY JENNY WHEAT

Buttercream Dreams

small cakes, big scoops, *and* sweet treats

Andrews McMeel
Publishing

Kansas City • Sydney • London

This book is dedicated to the three people in my life who have given me the inspiration for all of these crazy ideas! To my wife, *brandy*, who has encouraged me to follow my dreams and to take risks. Your unwavering support has made all of this possible, and I could not have done it without you by my side! For my daughter, *lily*, the inspiration behind the name that started it all. Your love for ice cream and cake makes me smile and reminds me every day that a cupcake does help! Just don't tell your mom how much we sneak when she's not looking! And to my little *jax*, those teeth are going to fall out anyway ... but keep brushing so we stay out of trouble with mom!

I would also like to thank all the Smallcakes staff, customers, and owners of our franchise locations. There isn't a day that goes by that I don't wake up and count myself lucky to be doing what I love and working with so many amazing people! I never dreamed that I'd be so fortunate to be writing a book, much less traveling the globe to assist other people in meeting their dreams as well. My story is the real American dream, and so I encourage everyone to take a risk and follow your own dreams ... you really can do anything you set your mind to!

Contents

INTRODUCTION

Life Is Sweet

Hi, my name is Jeff Martin, and I have the greatest job in the world. I am the founder of Smallcakes: A Cupcakery. Creating Smallcakes is an American-dream story. We started Smallcakes with very little money and a passion for bringing gourmet, amazing, delicious cupcakes to neighborhoods all over the country. I wanted to do this because cupcakes remind so many people of their cherished childhood memories of baking with Grandma and Mom.

People ask me all the time for our recipes or for advice on how to improve their own homemade cupcakes. This book represents everything I've learned after making thousands of cupcakes and other sweet treats. I'm excited to bring these cherished recipes to all of our fans and friends.

ABOUT SMALLCAKES:
MAYBE A CUPCAKE WILL HELP?

The history behind how we got started is definitely a modern-day entrepreneurial story. I worked in restaurants my whole life, but honestly, baking was never my forte. As I traveled to LA and NY, I noticed a few cupcake bakeries beginning to pop up. I was fascinated by them because all they served was cupcakes, yet they were extremely busy, but their product was average. I live in Kansas City where we really didn't have a "cupcake-only" bakery at the time. I told my wife my idea about opening a cupcake shop and she quickly shot it down because I'm not a baker. Eventually she came around and we started baking cupcakes at home to come up with a product that was better than what we had tried everywhere else. After all the cupcakes and frosting disasters, we finally found ten cupcake flavors that were amazing, including Cookies 'n' Cream Cupcakes (page 17), Orange Creamsicle Cupcakes (page 26), and Cinnamon Maple Cupcakes (page 23). As we were opening our first cupcake bakery, we also had a three-month-old baby girl named Lily, who would play a huge part in what we would become down the road.

When I started looking for a retail space, I met with many landlords who thought the idea of a cupcake bakery was not a smart one. After being turned down by five different landlords,

Our daughter, Lily's, nickname was "Smallcake."

we finally found one who said, "I don't think it's going to work, but I will lease you a space on a month-to-month basis."

When selecting a name for our shop, we considered just about everything. We wanted something that was unique and really conveyed to our customers who we were. After a few days of thinking and getting nowhere, we decided to take a drive. Our daughter, Lily's, nickname was "Smallcake." And as we were driving down the road talking to her, my wife leaned over and said, "Smallcakes is what we should name this crazy idea of a cupcake bakery." We painted the store using the colors of Lily's room, pink and brown. But with very little money, we had to decide between buying an oven for the store or buying a sign for the building. We chose to buy a sign and bake everything at home until we could afford to purchase an oven.

It was a Monday in June that we decided to open the doors. I baked the night before and took the cupcakes to our new bakery. When we opened at ten a.m., I had two ladies waiting at the front door. They walked in and looked around, asked a few questions, and then said, "This place is so cute, but it will never work with just cupcakes"—then left. Needless to say, I was a little nervous after that. But after two hours in business, I was out of cupcakes and driving

back to my house to make more. I did the same routine for a week until my wife said, "Let's buy an oven—I'm tired of my kitchen being dirty, and you are selling lots of cupcakes."

After six months of selling hundreds of cupcakes a day, my phone rang—it was a producer with the Food Network calling to discuss an upcoming reality show. After hanging up on her once because I thought it was a joke, she finally got it through to me that she was calling about the reality show *Cupcake Wars*. The show pits four bakeries against one another, challenging them to use crazy ingredients and produce hundreds of cupcakes during a limited amount of time. The winner takes home $10,000. I had never been on TV or been a reality TV fan, but I flew to Los Angles to participate in the show. It was season 1, and everything was crazy and changing at the last minute. That's TV!

During the first round of the show, I had to create a pumpkin cupcake with cardamom buttercream in forty-five minutes. Not knowing what cardamom was, I became a little concerned that my cupcake was not going to taste good. While I was trying to come up with a recipe, I had four TV cameras in my face watching everything I did. The producers were yelling to speak up or explain what I was doing. I knew I could make a great pumpkin cupcake, but the cardamom was what I was having trouble with. I made the pumpkin batter and put the cupcakes in the oven. I literally spent most of my time trying to get a phenomenal-tasting buttercream using this spice called cardamom. As the time was running out, the cupcakes were coming out of the oven. While they were cooling, my assistant looked at me and said, "I think you forgot to add something to the pumpkin cupcakes." We realized that I was

so worried about the cardamom buttercream that I forgot to add the pumpkin to the cake batter. I was so embarrassed and started freaking out about what I should do. I plated my cupcakes and took them up to the judges to be judged. There were three judges at the podium and they all took a bite and gave their critique. The funny thing was that all the judges loved the cake *and* the buttercream. They said it was the best cupcake they had had on the show that season. At that moment I had a choice to make: tell the truth about not using all my ingredients, or lie and see if I could make it to the next round. With cameras all around me, I decided to tell the truth. The judges were shocked but under the rules of the game I was voted off for not using all the ingredients.

Instead of going back home with my head down, I decided to make the best of what had

just happened to me. I had been on a national TV show, and that was a big deal. I started making T-shirts that said "I Forgot the Pumpkin." I took out billboards around town that had our Smallcakes logo and the phrase "I Forgot the Pumpkin." I really wanted everyone to know that the little cupcake store in Overland Park, Kansas, in a bad location, had just appeared on the Food Network. About a month after the show aired, I received a call from a producer for the daytime talk show *The View*. They wanted to feature us on their show as Whoopi's Favorite Desserts. There were only five cupcake bakeries there, and I was the only one not from Los Angeles or New York.

As the ladies from *The View* were going around tasting the cupcakes, Sherri Shepherd came to our table and took a bite of our Red Velvet Cupcake and said, "Now this is what a red velvet cupcake should taste like!" They also

recounted the episode of *Cupcake Wars* and how I had told the truth about not using the pumpkin in my cupcakes.

As all of this was happening in our lives, we grew from one store to three stores around the Kansas City area. The great part was every store had an oven. With the growth of the stores, we also grew as a family. Lily was getting older and we welcomed my son, Jax, into our lives. As we grew, we strived to stay very humbled by what was happening around us. On any given Saturday, you could find me and Lily at a store, baking and tasting the buttercream. We also grew from the ten core flavors we had started with to include S'mores, Blueberry, and Key Lime Cupcakes (page 21). Our menu grew to where we were offering fifteen flavors every day. The great thing about cupcakes and other sweet treats is that you can put your own new twist on old flavors. One of my favorite recipes in this book is the Caramel Pecan Carrot Cupcakes (page 7). My grandmother always made this as a cake. When I was looking for recipes to create for the store, I looked at the past and tried to think about what I could do differently to make it better or give it a new, modern twist. These cupcakes are amazing—and what I do differently than Grandma is add crushed pineapple and a little extra cinnamon.

We started franchising in 2009 and have grown to ninety locations in seventeen states, as well as internationally. As we continued to grow, we started thinking of ways to be different from the other cupcake bakeries. We created our own ice cream and other sweet treats, which you'll also find in this book. Our ice cream reflects the old-school creamy and rich-tasting flavors. Salted Caramel Ice Cream (page 58) is one of my favorites. It starts with salt, heavy cream, and eggs, just like they used to do back in the day. This book also contains recipes for personal family favorites including Mom's Holiday Fudge (page 73).

Even though we are a growing company, we try to keep things simple and small and not forget where we started. I still create a lot of our recipes today, along with our amazing owners, and draw inspiration from my kids. While spending time together, we come up with ideas. Some have been hits, like Jax's Bubble Gum Cupcakes (page 33) and Lily's Strawberry Ice Cream (page 57). I try to use the freshest ingredients in our products and encourage you to do the same as you are enjoying this book. I hope you enjoy the adventure and find that a cupcake or other sweet treat *really* does make the day better.

Small Cakes

cupcakes

1½ cups sugar

1 cup unsweetened cocoa powder

1 cup all-purpose flour

½ cup sifted cake flour

2 tablespoons malted milk powder

1½ teaspoons baking powder

1 teaspoon baking soda

½ teaspoon salt

1 cup (2 sticks) unsalted butter,
at room temperature

4 large eggs

1 cup nonfat Greek yogurt

2 teaspoons pure vanilla extract

black-and-white malt frosting

4 ounces semisweet chocolate, chopped

6 egg whites

2 cups sugar

2 cups (4 sticks) unsalted butter,
at room temperature

½ cup malted milk powder

2 teaspoons vanilla bean paste

1 cup malted milk balls, for garnish

CHOCOLATE MALTED MILK BALL CUPCAKES

Malt balls take you back to your childhood. It's that chocolate taste on a hot summer day hanging with friends. I wanted to make a classic cupcake using a classic candy.

MAKES 12 CUPCAKES

1. To make the cupcakes, preheat the oven to 350°F. Line a 12-cup muffin tin with paper cupcake liners.

2. In a large bowl, combine the sugar, cocoa powder, all-purpose flour, cake flour, malted milk powder, baking powder, baking soda, and salt. Add the butter and stir until the mixture resembles damp sand.

3. Add the eggs, one at a time, scraping the bottom and sides of the bowl with a spatula after each addition. Stir in the yogurt and vanilla and scrape the bowl again.

4. Using an electric mixer, beat on medium speed for about 1½ minutes to aerate the batter and build the cake's structure. It will be thick—you should be able to make a figure eight in the batter.

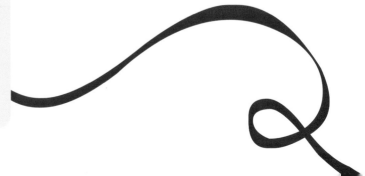

5. Fill each cupcake liner two-thirds full with batter. Bake for 15 minutes, until a toothpick inserted into the center of a cupcake comes out clean or with a few moist crumbs. Let cool completely on a wire rack before frosting.

6. To make the frosting, place the chocolate in the top section of a double boiler and melt over medium-low heat. Alternatively, place the chocolate in a microwave-safe bowl and microwave on medium for 30-second increments at a time until the chocolate has melted. Set aside.

7. Place the egg whites and sugar in a large metal or glass bowl and whisk to combine. Set the bowl over a pot of simmering water, making sure the bottom of the bowl does not touch the water, and cook, whisking occasionally, until the sugar has dissolved. (The mixture should no longer feel gritty when rubbed between your thumb and forefinger.)Remove the bowl from the heat, and whip on high speed until stiff peaks form. Add the butter, a tablespoon at a time, while continuing to whip. Stir in the malted milk powder and vanilla bean paste.

8. Divide the buttercream equally between two bowls and fold the melted chocolate into one bowl. Transfer the vanilla and chocolate buttercreams to separate pastry bags fitted with plain, circular tips. Alternatively, transfer them to resealable plastic bags and snip off one corner of each bag for piping. Pipe the buttercream onto the cupcakes, swirling the vanilla and chocolate together. Garnish the cupcakes with malted milk balls. Store in an airtight container in the refrigerator for up to 3 days.

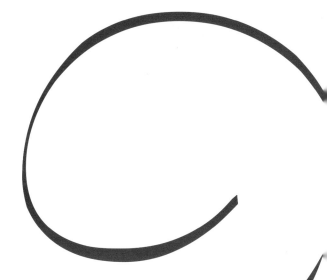

cupcakes

10 to 12 bacon slices

1½ cups all-purpose flour

1½ teaspoons baking powder

½ teaspoon ground cinnamon

¼ teaspoon salt

½ cup (1 stick) unsalted butter, melted and cooled

1 cup granulated sugar

2 large eggs

1 teaspoon maple extract

½ cup whole milk

maple buttercream

¾ cup (1½ sticks) unsalted butter, at room temperature

2 tablespoons pure maple syrup

½ teaspoon maple extract

Pinch of salt

2 cups confectioners' sugar

FRENCH TOAST AND BACON CUPCAKES

Breakfast in a cupcake, what could be better? This recipe was created because my daughter's favorite breakfast is French toast and bacon. She was delighted with this surprise on her breakfast plate one morning.

MAKES 12 CUPCAKES

1. To make the cupcakes, preheat the oven to 350°F. Line a 12-cup muffin tin with paper cupcake liners. Line a plate with paper towels.

2. Using your preferred method, cook the bacon in batches until browned and still slightly flexible, but not too crispy. Transfer to the paper towel–lined plate and set aside to cool. Once the bacon is cool enough to handle, cut twelve 1-inch-long pieces of bacon—this will be the garnish for each cupcake. Set aside. Chop or tear the remaining bacon into tiny pieces and set aside.

3. In a small bowl, mix together the flour, baking powder, cinnamon, and salt. Set aside.

4. In a large bowl, whisk together the butter, granulated sugar, and eggs until smooth. Whisk in the maple extract. In alternating additions, whisk in the flour mixture and the milk, beginning with the flour and scraping down the bowl after each addition. Beat until smooth. Fold in the small bacon pieces until evenly distributed throughout the batter.

continued on page 6

FRENCH TOAST AND BACON CUPCAKES
CONTINUED

5. Fill each cupcake liner three-quarters full with batter. Bake for 20 to 25 minutes, until the cupcakes are golden brown and the tops spring back when touched lightly. Let cool in the pan on a wire rack for 10 minutes, then remove from the pan and let cool completely before frosting.

6. To make the maple buttercream, in a large bowl using a hand mixer, beat the butter until light and fluffy. Add the maple syrup, maple extract, and salt and beat until well combined. Add the confectioners' sugar, ½ cup at a time, and beat until smooth and fluffy, about 5 minutes.

7. Using a table knife or spatula, swirl the buttercream on top of each cupcake, or transfer the buttercream to a pastry bag fitted with a plain tip and pipe it onto the cupcakes. Top each with a bacon piece. Store in an airtight container in the refrigerator for up to 3 days.

cupcakes

1 cup granulated sugar

1 cup all-purpose flour

1 teaspoon baking soda

½ teaspoon salt

1½ teaspoons ground cinnamon

¾ cup canola or vegetable oil

2 large eggs, beaten

1 teaspoon pure vanilla extract

1 cup finely shredded carrots

½ cup crushed pineapple, well drained

½ cup raisins (optional)

½ cup chopped pecans

cream cheese frosting

½ cup (1 stick) unsalted butter,
at room temperature

1¾ cups confectioners' sugar

⅛ teaspoon salt

2 teaspoons pure vanilla extract

1 (8-ounce) package cream
cheese, at room temperature

¼ cup store-bought caramel
topping, for garnish

¼ cup pecans, chopped, for garnish

CARAMEL PECAN CARROT CUPCAKES

My grandmother always made us pick up pecans in her yard and then crack them for this cake. It was my childhood favorite and reminds me of home in the South. It was originally a cake recipe that we changed into a cupcake recipe.

MAKES 12 CUPCAKES

1. To make the cupcakes, preheat the oven to 350°F. Line a 12-cup muffin tin with paper cupcake liners.

2. In a large bowl, combine the granulated sugar, flour, baking soda, salt, and cinnamon. Add the oil, eggs, and vanilla and mix well. Stir in the carrots, pineapple, raisins (if using), and pecans until combined.

3. Fill each cupcake liner three-quarters full with batter. Bake for 15 to 16 minutes, until the cupcakes are golden brown. Let cool completely on a wire rack before frosting.

4. To make the cream cheese frosting, in the bowl of a stand mixer or in a large bowl using a hand mixer, cream together the butter, confectioners' sugar, and salt, starting at low speed and gradually increasing to high, until the mixture becomes light and fluffy (the butter-sugar mixture takes about 2 minutes to come together). Add the cream cheese, 2 ounces at a time, and beat for 2 minutes more, scraping down the bowl as needed.

5. Using a table knife or spatula, swirl the frosting on top of each cupcake. Using a spoon, drizzle the caramel over the tops of the frosted cupcakes. Sprinkle with the pecans. Store in an airtight container in the refrigerator for up to 3 days.

cupcakes

1 cup whole wheat pastry flour

1 cup all-purpose flour

½ cup sifted coconut milk powder

1 teaspoon baking powder

½ teaspoon salt

1¼ cups (2½ sticks) unsalted butter, at room temperature

1 (8-ounce) package cream cheese, at room temperature

1½ cups granulated sugar

½ teaspoon pure vanilla extract

4 drops coconut flavoring, or ¾ teaspoon coconut extract

5 large eggs

2 tablespoons whole milk

1¾ cups bittersweet chocolate chips

ingredients continued

COCONUT–CHOCOLATE CHIP CUPCAKES

The addition of coconut milk powder to the cake and frosting adds a little island feel to a classic cupcake. A double dose of coconut with chocolate is outstanding.

MAKES 12 CUPCAKES

1. To make the cupcakes, preheat the oven to 350°F. Line a 12-cup muffin tin with paper cupcake liners.

2. In a medium bowl, sift together the whole wheat pastry flour, all-purpose flour, coconut milk powder, baking powder, and salt. Set aside.

3. In a large bowl, use a hand mixer to beat the butter and cream cheese until smooth. Gradually beat in the sugar, then the vanilla extract and coconut flavoring. Beat in the sifted dry ingredients. (The batter will be stiff.) Add the eggs one at a time, beating until each is incorporated before adding the next. Beat in the milk and then stir in the chocolate chips.

4. Fill each cupcake liner three-quarters full with batter. Bake for 20 to 22 minutes, until a toothpick inserted into the center of a cupcake comes out clean. Let cool completely on a wire rack before frosting.

continued

coconut frosting

½ cup (1 stick) unsalted butter, at room temperature

½ cup coconut milk powder (sifted, then measured)

¼ teaspoon salt

½ teaspoon pure vanilla extract

3 drops coconut flavoring or ½ teaspoon coconut extract

5 cups confectioners' sugar

4 tablespoons whole milk

Flaked sweetened coconut, for garnish

COCONUT–CHOCOLATE CHIP CUPCAKES
CONTINUED

5. To make the coconut frosting, in a large bowl, use a hand mixer to beat the butter, coconut milk powder, and salt until smooth. Beat in the vanilla and coconut flavoring. Beat in the confectioners' sugar, 1 cup at a time, to form very a thick frosting. Beat in the milk, 1 tablespoon at a time, until the frosting is thin enough to spread.

6. Transfer the frosting to a pastry bag fitted with a plain tip and pipe a swirl of frosting on top of each cupcake. Garnish each with a sprinkle of coconut. Store in an airtight container at room temperature for up to 3 days.

cupcakes

2½ cups cake flour

1 teaspoon salt

2 cups granulated sugar

1 cup (2 sticks) unsalted butter,
at room temperature

2 large eggs

2 tablespoons unsweetened
cocoa powder

1 ounce red food coloring

1 cup regular buttermilk

1 teaspoon pure vanilla extract

½ teaspoon baking soda

1 tablespoon distilled white vinegar

cream cheese—marshmallow frosting

1 (8-ounce) package cream cheese

½ cup (1 stick) unsalted butter,
at room temperature

2 cups mini marshmallows, melted

3 to 4 cups confectioners' sugar

FAMOUS RED VELVET
CUPCAKES

This is our most popular flavor. It gained popularity when Sherri Shepherd from the hit daytime talk show *The View* said it was the best she'd ever had. It's a recipe from my wife's grandmother and one of the original signature flavors we started with.

MAKES 12 CUPCAKES

1. To make the cupcakes, preheat the oven to 350°F. Line a 12-cup muffin tin with paper cupcake liners.

2. In a medium bowl, sift together the flour and salt. Set aside.

3. In a large bowl using a hand mixer, cream together the granulated sugar and butter until light and fluffy. Add the eggs one at a time, beating until each is incorporated before adding the next.

4. In a small bowl, stir together the cocoa powder and food coloring. Add the cocoa mixture to the butter-sugar mixture and mix well.

continued

FAMOUS RED VELVET CUPCAKES
CONTINUED

5. In alternating additions, add the flour mixture and the buttermilk to the butter-sugar mixture, stirring well to combine after each addition. Blend in the vanilla.

6. In a small bowl, stir together the baking soda and vinegar. Add the baking soda mixture to the batter.

7. Fill each cupcake liner three-quarters full with batter. Bake for 15 to 20 minutes, until a toothpick inserted into the center of a cupcake comes out clean. Let cool completely on a wire rack before frosting.

8. To make the cream cheese–marshmallow frosting, in a large bowl, stir together the cream cheese and butter. Add the melted marshmallows and confectioners' sugar and blend.

9. Transfer the frosting to a pastry bag fitted with a plain tip and pipe a swirl of frosting on top of each cupcake. Store in an airtight container in the refrigerator for up to 3 days.

cupcakes

1⅔ cups all-purpose flour

½ teaspoon baking powder

¼ teaspoon baking soda

½ teaspoon salt

1 cup granulated sugar

½ cup (1 stick) unsalted butter, melted

2 large egg whites

¼ cup vanilla Greek yogurt

¾ cup vanilla almond milk

2 teaspoons pure vanilla extract

⅛ cup sprinkles

vanilla bean frosting

1 cup (2 sticks) unsalted butter,
at room temperature

4 cups confectioners' sugar

¼ cup heavy cream

1 teaspoon pure vanilla extract

1 tablespoon vanilla bean paste

Sprinkles, for garnish

RAINBOW AND
SPRINKLE CUPCAKES

Kids love sprinkles. And they love colorful rainbows. So we decided to give them both together in one of our original signature flavors.

MAKES 12 CUPCAKES

1. To make the cupcakes, preheat the oven to 350°F. Line a 12-cup muffin tin with paper cupcake liners.

2. In a medium bowl, stir together the flour, baking powder, baking soda, and salt until combined. Set aside.

3. In a large bowl, whisk the granulated sugar into the melted butter; the mixture will be gritty. Stir in the egg whites, yogurt, almond milk, and vanilla extract until combined.

4. Slowly add the flour mixture to the sugar mixture, stirring until no lumps remain. Stir the sprinkles into the batter.

It's colorful, it's fun, and it's every kid's favorite flavor.

continued

5. Fill each cupcake liner three-quarters full with batter. Bake for 23 to 25 minutes, until a toothpick inserted into the center of a cupcake comes out clean. Let cool completely on a wire rack before frosting.

6. To make the vanilla bean frosting, in a large bowl using a hand mixer, beat the butter on medium speed for about 3 minutes, until smooth and creamy. With the mixer running, add the confectioners' sugar, cream, vanilla extract, and vanilla bean paste. Raise the speed to high and beat for 3 minutes.

7. Transfer the frosting to a pastry bag fitted with a plain tip and pipe a swirl of frosting on top of each cupcake. Top with sprinkles. Store in an airtight container in the refrigerator for up to 3 days.

cupcakes

1⅔ cups all-purpose flour

½ teaspoon baking powder

¼ teaspoon baking soda

½ teaspoon salt

1 cup granulated sugar

½ cup (1 stick) unsalted butter, melted

2 large egg whites

¼ cup vanilla Greek yogurt

¾ cup whole milk

2 teaspoons pure vanilla extract

1½ cups chopped chocolate sandwich cookies (from 14 to 15 cookies)

milk chocolate frosting

1 cup (2 sticks) unsalted butter, at room temperature

3½ cups confectioners' sugar, divided

½ cup unsweetened cocoa powder

½ teaspoon salt

2 teaspoons pure vanilla extract

3 tablespoons heavy cream

4 to 5 crumbled chocolate sandwich cookies, for garnish

COOKIES 'N' CREAM
CUPCAKES

Imagine little pieces of your favorite chocolate sandwich cookies hidden in an awesomely rich cupcake. This was the very first recipe we created in our kitchen at home. It's available in all our stores and is a fan favorite.

MAKES 12 CUPCAKES

1. To make the cupcakes, preheat the oven to 350°F. Line a 12-cup muffin tin with paper cupcake liners.

2. In a large bowl, stir together the flour, baking powder, baking soda, and salt until combined. Set aside.

3. In a medium bowl, whisk the granulated sugar into the melted butter; the mixture will be thick and gritty. Vigorously whisk in the egg whites, yogurt, milk, and vanilla extract until combined and uniform in texture. Slowly whisk the sugar mixture into the flour mixture until no lumps remain. Gently fold in the chocolate sandwich cookies.

4. Fill each cupcake liner three-quarters full with batter. Bake for 20 to 24 minutes, until a toothpick inserted into the center of a cupcake comes out clean. Let cool completely on a wire rack before frosting.

continued

5. To make the milk chocolate frosting, in a large bowl using a hand mixer, beat the butter on medium speed for 3 to 4 minutes.

6. With the mixer on low speed, slowly incorporate 3 cups of the confectioners' sugar, the cocoa powder, and the salt. Mix until all the dry ingredients have been absorbed by the butter. Raise the mixer speed to medium and add the vanilla.

7. Slowly add the cream and beat for about 2 minutes, or until the frosting reaches the desired thickness. Add the remaining ½ cup confectioners' sugar if needed to increase the frosting's thickness.

8. Using a table knife or spatula, swirl the frosting on top of each cupcake. Top each with a few chocolate sandwich cookie crumbles. Store in an airtight container in the refrigerator for up to 3 days.

cupcakes

3 cups all-purpose flour

1 tablespoon baking powder

½ teaspoon salt

1 cup (2 sticks) unsalted butter

2 cups granulated sugar

6 large eggs

½ cup whole milk

2 tablespoons finely grated key lime zest

key lime curd

3 large eggs

¾ cup granulated sugar

¼ cup fresh key lime juice

1 tablespoon finely grated key lime zest

4 tablespoon (½ stick) unsalted butter, cold

ingredients continued

KEY LIME
CUPCAKES

My family and I love spending a lot of time in Florida. When we can't be there, this recipe takes us back to that beach town and memories of sandy feet. The double dose of key lime in both the cupcake and the frosting will have you hearing the ocean in no time.

MAKES 12 CUPCAKES

1. To make the cupcakes, preheat the oven to 300°F. Line a 12-cup muffin tin with paper cupcake liners.

2. In a large bowl, sift together the flour, baking powder, and salt. Set aside.

3. In the bowl of a stand mixer fitted with the paddle attachment, cream together the butter and granulated sugar for about 2 minutes. Scrape down the bowl and add the eggs, one at a time, beating well after each addition before incorporating the next. Scrape down the bowl and add the milk and lime zest, then add the flour mixture and mix on low until well incorporated. Scrape down the bowl and raise the mixer speed to medium and mix for about 20 seconds. Scrape down the bowl a final time.

4. Fill each cupcake liner three-quarters full with batter. Bake for 20 to 22 minutes, until a toothpick inserted into the center of a cupcake comes out clean. Let cool completely on a wire rack before filling and frosting.

continued

key lime–cream cheese frosting

1 cup (2 sticks) unsalted butter

1 (8-ounce) package cream cheese, at room temperature

5 to 6 cups confectioners' sugar, sifted

2 tablespoons finely grated key lime zest

2 tablespoons fresh key lime juice

12 key lime slices, for garnish

5. To make the key lime curd, in a stainless-steel bowl, whisk together the eggs, granulated sugar, and lime juice. Set aside.

6. Fill a small saucepan halfway with water and bring to a simmer over medium-high heat. Place the bowl with the egg mixture over the pan, making sure the bottom of the bowl does not touch the water. Cook, stirring with a spatula, until the mixture is creamy (like sour cream), 6 to 8 minutes. Remove the bowl from the heat and strain the custard through a fine-mesh strainer into a bowl, getting rid of any curdled egg. Add the lime zest and butter and stir until well incorporated. Cover and refrigerate until slightly thickened, 10 to 15 minutes.

7. To make the key lime–cream cheese frosting, in the bowl of a stand mixer fitted with the paddle attachment, cream together the butter and cream cheese on low speed. Scrape down the bowl and add the sifted confectioners' sugar, 1 cup at a time. Slowly add the lime zest and juice until well incorporated. Scrape down the bowl and mix on low speed. Raise the speed to high and mix for about 2 minutes more, until creamy and fluffy.

8. To assemble the cupcakes, make a hollow in the center of each cupcake with an apple corer or melon baller and set aside. Fill the hollow with the curd. Transfer the frosting to a pastry bag fitted with a ½-inch plain tip and pipe a swirl of frosting on top of each cupcake. Top with a slice of lime. Store in an airtight container in the refrigerator for up to 3 days.

cupcakes

1⅔ cups all-purpose flour

1¼ cups granulated sugar, divided

2 tablespoons ground cinnamon, divided

¼ teaspoon baking soda

1 teaspoon baking powder

¾ cup (1½ sticks) unsalted butter, at room temperature

3 large egg whites

2 teaspoons pure vanilla extract

½ cup sour cream

½ cup milk

cinnamon maple frosting

½ cup vegetable shortening

½ cup (1 stick) unsalted butter

4 cups confectioners' sugar, divided

2½ teaspoons ground cinnamon

¾ teaspoon maple extract

1 to 2 tablespoons milk

CINNAMON MAPLE
CUPCAKES

I love cinnamon maple French toast and thought it would make a great addition to our cupcake family. The old saying is "breakfast of champions!"

MAKES 12 CUPCAKES

1. To make the cupcakes, preheat the oven to 350°F. Line a 12-cup muffin tin with paper cupcake liners.

2. In a large bowl, whisk together the flour, 1 cup of the granulated sugar, a ½ tablespoon of the cinnamon, the baking soda, and the baking powder. Add the butter, egg whites, vanilla, sour cream, and milk and beat on medium speed until smooth.

3. In a small bowl, combine the remaining 1½ tablespoons cinnamon and the remaining ¼ cup granulated sugar.

4. Fill each cupcake liner three-quarters full of batter. Sprinkle ¼ teaspoon of the cinnamon sugar on top of each cupcake. Bake for 16 to 18 minutes, until a toothpick inserted into the center of a cupcake comes out with just a few crumbs. Let cool completely on a wire rack before frosting.

continued

CINNAMON MAPLE CUPCAKES
CONTINUED

5. To make the cinnamon maple frosting, in a large bowl using a hand mixer, beat together the shortening and butter until smooth.

6. Slowly add 3 cups of the confectioner's sugar and mix until combined. Mix in the cinnamon, maple extract, and 1 to 2 tablespoons of milk until smooth. Slowly add the remaining 1 cup confectioners' sugar and mix until smooth.

7. Transfer the frosting to a pastry bag fitted with a plain tip and pipe a swirl of frosting on top of each cupcake. Store in an airtight container in the refrigerator for up to 3 days.

cupcakes

1½ cups all-purpose flour

½ cup sliced almonds

2 teaspoons baking powder

½ cup (1 stick) unsalted butter

⅔ cup granulated sugar

2 large eggs

1 teaspoon pure vanilla extract

½ teaspoon almond extract

⅔ cup buttermilk

vanilla frosting

2 tablespoons unsalted butter

2 cups confectioners' sugar

2 tablespoons milk

1 teaspoon pure vanilla extract

¼ teaspoon almond extract

VANILLA ALMOND CUPCAKES

This is our version of a wedding cake cupcake. The vanilla and almond complement each other. It's a rather light cupcake and the vanilla frosting can be used on almost any flavor of cupcake.

MAKES 12 CUPCAKES

1. To make the cupcakes, preheat the oven to 350°F. Line a 12-cup muffin tin with paper cupcake liners.

2. In a large bowl, whisk together the flour, almonds, and baking powder. Set aside.

3. In a separate large bowl using a hand mixer, cream together the butter and granulated sugar until light and fluffy. Add the eggs one at a time, beating well after each addition before adding the next. Beat in the vanilla and almond extracts. In three alternate additions, add the flour mixture and the buttermilk, blending until smooth after each addition.

4. Fill each cupcake liner three-quarters full of batter. Bake for 18 to 22 minutes, until a toothpick inserted into the center of a cupcake comes out clean. Let cool completely on a wire rack before frosting.

5. To make the vanilla frosting, in a medium bowl using a hand mixer, beat together the butter and confectioners' sugar until combined. Add the milk, vanilla extract, and almond extract and beat until the mixture is light and fluffy.

6. Transfer the frosting to a pastry bag fitted with a plain tip and pipe a swirl of frosting on top of each cupcake. Store in an airtight container in the refrigerator for up to 3 days.

cupcakes

2 cups all-purpose flour

¼ teaspoon baking powder

¼ teaspoon baking soda

¼ teaspoon salt

½ cup butter, at room temperature

1 cup granulated sugar

1½ tablespoons finely grated orange zest (from about 1½ oranges)

2 large eggs

¾ cup heavy cream (for lighter texture use half-and-half)

¼ cup orange juice, freshly squeezed

1½ teaspoons orange extract

1 teaspoon pure vanilla extract

orange buttercream

3 cups confectioners' sugar

1 cup (2 sticks) unsalted butter

1 teaspoon pure vanilla extract

1 to 2 tablespoons heavy cream

1 tablespoon orange extract

¼ teaspoon orange food coloring

12 thin orange slices, for garnish

ORANGE CREAMSICLE
CUPCAKES

This summer favorite will remind you of the bell of the ice cream truck coming through the neighborhood. The one thing better about this version is you don't have to worry about the sun melting it away so fast—you can slowly savor the creamy orange goodness.

MAKES 12 CUPCAKES

1. To make the cupcakes, preheat the oven to 350°F. Line a 12-cup muffin tin with paper cupcake liners.

2. In a large bowl, whisk together the flour, baking powder, baking soda, and salt. Set aside.

3. In a large bowl using a hand mixer, blend together the butter, sugar, and orange zest on medium-high speed until pale and fluffy, about 3 to 4 minutes. Mix in the eggs one at time, blending well after each addition.

4. Measure the cream into a liquid measuring cup, and stir in the orange juice, orange extract, and vanilla extract. With a hand mixer on low speed, work in three separate batches, blending in the flour mixture alternating with the cream mixture. Be sure to begin and end with the flour mixture. Mix just until combined after each addition.

continued on page 28

ORANGE CREAMSICLE CUPCAKES
CONTINUED

5. Fill each cup three-quarters full with batter. Bake for 23 to 25 minutes, rotating the muffin tin once halfway through baking, until a toothpick inserted into the center of a cupcake comes out clean. Let cool several minutes before transferring to a wire rack. Let cool completely before frosting.

6. To make the orange buttercream, in a stand mixer fitted with the whisk attachment, mix together the confectioners' sugar and butter. Mix on low speed until well blended and then increase the speed to medium and beat for another 3 minutes.

7. Add the vanilla, cream, orange extract, and orange food coloring and continue to beat on medium speed for 1 minute more, adding more cream for the desired consistency if needed.

8. Transfer the frosting to a pastry bag fitted with a plain tip and pipe a swirl of frosting on top of each cupcake. Garnish with a small orange slice just before serving. Store in an airtight container at room temperature for up to 3 days.

cupcakes

1⅓ cups all-purpose flour

1¾ cups granulated sugar

¾ teaspoon baking powder

½ teaspoon baking soda

¾ cup cocoa powder

⅔ cup brewed coffee, scalding hot

⅔ cup regular buttermilk

⅓ cup canola oil

1 teaspoon pure vanilla extract

1 large egg

1 large egg yolk

½ teaspoon salt

peanut butter buttercream

1 cup (2 sticks) unsalted butter, at room temperature

1 cup smooth peanut butter (don't use natural)

1½ cups confectioners' sugar

¼ teaspoon salt

½ teaspoon pure vanilla extract

1 to 2 tablespoons heavy cream or whole milk

ingredients continued

CHOCOLATE–PEANUT BUTTER PRETZEL CUPCAKES

My son loves chocolate pretzels and one day at our bakery he dipped his chocolate pretzel in peanut butter. It tasted so good so we decided to take his lead and turn this combination into a cupcake.

MAKES 12 CUPCAKES

1. To make the cupcakes, preheat the oven to 350°F. Line a 12-cup muffin tin with paper cupcake liners.

2. In a medium bowl, sift together the flour, granulated sugar, baking powder, and baking soda. Set aside.

3. Place the cocoa powder in the bowl of a stand mixer fitted with the paddle attachment. Pour the hot coffee over the cocoa. Mix on low speed until a thick paste forms and the mixture stops steaming, about 1 minute.

4. In a 4-cup measuring cup, combine the buttermilk, oil, vanilla, egg, egg yolk, and salt and mix lightly with a fork, ensuring the yolks are broken. Raise the mixer speed to medium and slowly pour in the buttermilk mixture.

continued

classic ganache

¼ cup chopped semisweet chocolate

¼ cup heavy cream

Pinch of sea salt

1½ cups salted pretzels rods or other thick pretzels, for garnish

¾ cup roasted peanuts, for garnish

CHOCOLATE–PEANUT BUTTER PRETZEL CUPCAKES
CONTINUED

5. Stop the mixer and scrape the bottom of the bowl well to loosen any caked-on cocoa. Beat the batter on medium speed for 1 minute. Add the flour mixture to the batter and mix on low speed until just combined. Remove the bowl and paddle and scrape down the sides of the bowl, ensuring everything is mixed.

6. Fill each cupcake liner two-thirds full with batter. Bake for 20 to 25 minute. The cupcakes are done when the centers spring back when you touch them. Let cool completely on a wire rack before frosting.

7. To make the peanut butter buttercream, in the bowl of a stand mixer fitted with the whisk attachment, beat the butter and peanut butter on medium-high speed until smooth, about 20 seconds.

8. Add the confectioners' sugar and salt and beat on medium-low speed for about 45 seconds, until the sugar is moistened. Scrape down the sides of the bowl and then mix on medium speed until the sugar is fully incorporated, about 15 seconds.

9. Add the vanilla and cream and beat on medium speed until combined, about 10 seconds. Raise the speed to medium-high and beat until light and fluffy, about 4 minutes, scraping down the bowl a few times during mixing. Set aside until ready to frost the cupcakes.

10. To make the classic ganache, place the chocolate in a bowl. In a medium saucepan, combine the cream and sea salt and bring to a boil over medium heat. Immediately pour the hot cream mixture over the chocolate in the bowl and let sit for 2 minutes to allow the chocolate to melt. Using a heatproof spatula, stir the cream and chocolate together until completely smooth.

11. Allow the ganache to slightly cool before using. It should not be hot to the touch, but should still be liquid. If it cools completely and becomes solid, microwave it for 20 seconds, stirring until the desired consistency is reached.

12. To assemble the cupcakes, transfer the frosting to a pastry bag fitted with a plain tip and pipe a swirl of frosting on top of each cupcake.

13. Pulse the pretzels and peanuts in a food processor until they're coarse crumbs. Place the crumbs in a pie dish or baking pan.

14. Take the cupcakes and gently roll the sides of the buttercream in the pretzel mixture. Pour a handful of the mixture over the top of each cupcake and lightly pack on by hand. Shake off any excess and set aside. Drizzle a small amount of the ganache across each cupcake. Store in an airtight container in the refrigerator for up to 3 days.

cupcakes

½ cup heavy cream

2½ cups cake flour

1 tablespoon baking powder

½ teaspoon sea salt

1 cup whole milk

1 teaspoon pure vanilla extract

3 large egg whites, at
room temperature

½ cup (1 stick) unsalted butter,
at room temperature

1½ cups granulated sugar

2 tablespoons bubble gum
extract (see headnote)

bubble gum frosting

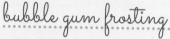

1 cup (2 sticks) unsalted butter,
at room temperature

1 (8-ounce) package cream
cheese, at room temperature

4 to 5 cups confectioners' sugar, divided

3 tablespoons heavy cream

2 teaspoons pure vanilla extract

3 tablespoons bubble gum extract

12 colorful gum balls, for garnish

JAX'S BUBBLE GUM
CUPCAKES

My son, Jax, loves chewing bubble gum. One day in a candy store, he asked if he could have his very own special cupcake like his sister. The flavor in the cupcake and matching frosting doesn't come from actual chewing gum, but from bubble gum extract that you can purchase at any craft store or cake decorating shop. It comes in both blue and pink, depending upon your preference.

MAKES 12 CUPCAKES

1. To make the cupcakes, preheat the oven to 350°F. Line a 12-cup muffin tin with paper cupcake liners.

2. Chill a medium bowl in the freezer for 5 minutes. Using a hand mixer, beat the cream in the chilled bowl until soft peaks form. Refrigerate until ready to use.

3. In a medium bowl, sift together the flour, baking powder, and salt. Set aside.

4. In a separate medium bowl, whisk together the milk, vanilla, and egg whites.

continued

5. In a stand mixer fitted with the paddle attachment, cream together the butter and granulated sugar on medium speed until very creamy, about 5 minutes.

6. With the mixer running on medium speed, alternate between adding the flour mixture and the milk mixture. Blend until well incorporated.

7. Add the bubble gum extract and mix well, then continue mixing on medium for 2 minutes more. Using a rubber spatula, gently fold the whipped cream into the cake batter.

8. Fill each cupcake liner two-thirds full of batter. Bake for 15 to 16 minutes, until a toothpick inserted into the center of a cupcake comes out clean. Let cool completely on a wire rack before frosting.

9. To make the bubble gum frosting, in a large bowl using a hand mixer, beat together the butter and cream cheese until creamy. Slowly add the confectioners' sugar, 1 cup at a time. After 2 to 3 cups, add the heavy cream, vanilla, and bubble gum extract. Add the remaining confectioners' sugar and beat for 5 minutes more, until light and fluffy.

10. Transfer the frosting to a pastry bag fitted with a plain tip and pipe a swirl of frosting on top of each cupcake. Top each with a colorful gum ball. Store in an airtight container in the refrigerator for up to 3 days.

cupcakes

2½ cups all-purpose flour

1½ teaspoons baking powder

½ teaspoon baking soda

½ teaspoon salt

3 large eggs

1¾ cups granulated sugar

1 cup vegetable oil

1 teaspoon pure vanilla extract

¾ cup sour cream

1½ cups canned crushed pineapple, drained slightly

coconut–cream cheese frosting

½ cup (1 stick) unsalted butter

1 (8-ounce) package cream cheese

½ teaspoon pure vanilla extract

1½ teaspoons coconut extract

4 cups confectioners' sugar

1 tablespoon heavy cream

1 tablespoon dark rum (optional)

Toasted coconut, for garnish

12 colorful paper umbrellas, for garnish

NAOMI'S PINEAPPLE CUPCAKES

This is a favorite summer cupcake, great for summer holidays. Having a summer birthday, this cupcake is what I always wanted as my birthday cake. Once you bite into it, you get that sweet summer taste. And who doesn't love a cupcake with an umbrella in it?

MAKES 12 CUPCAKES

1. To make the cupcakes, preheat the oven to 350°F. Line a 12-cup muffin tin with paper cupcake liners.

2. In a medium bowl, stir together the flour, baking powder, baking soda, and salt. Set aside.

3. In a large bowl using a hand mixer, beat the eggs and granulated sugar on medium speed until slightly thickened and a light cream color, about 2 minutes. On low speed, mix in the oil and vanilla until blended.

4. Add the sour cream and pineapple and gently mix until fully incorporated. Add the flour mixture and mix until just combined and smooth.

continued

5. Fill each cupcake liner two-thirds full of batter. Bake for 22 minutes, until a toothpick inserted into the center of a cupcake comes out clean. Let cool completely on a wire rack before frosting.

6. To make the coconut–cream cheese frosting, in a large bowl using a hand mixer, beat the butter until smooth. Add the cream cheese and beat until well combined, about 30 seconds.

7. Add the vanilla and coconut extract. Add the confectioners' sugar, 1 cup at a time, and blend on low speed until combined. Raise the speed to medium and beat until the batter begins to get fluffy.

8. Slowly add the heavy cream and the rum (if using). Beat until fluffy, about 1 minute.

9. Transfer the frosting to a pastry bag fitted with a plain tip and pipe a swirl of frosting on top of each cupcake. Top with a few sprinkles of toasted coconut and an umbrella. Store in an airtight container in the refrigerator for up to 3 days.

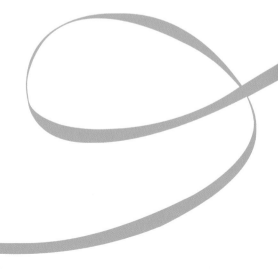

cupcakes

1 cup all-purpose flour

1 teaspoon ground cinnamon

½ teaspoon ground ginger

½ teaspoon ground allspice

½ teaspoon freshly grated nutmeg

½ teaspoon baking powder

½ teaspoon baking soda

¼ teaspoon salt

½ cup (1 stick) unsalted butter, at room temperature

½ cup granulated sugar

½ cup canned pure pumpkin purée

1½ teaspoons pure vanilla extract

2 large eggs

cardamom buttercream

1 cup (2 sticks) unsalted butter, at room temperature

1 tablespoon pure vanilla extract

2 teaspoons ground cardamom

¼ cup whole milk

5 cups confectioners' sugar, sifted

INFAMOUS PUMPKIN CUPCAKES WITH CARDAMOM BUTTERCREAM

On the show *Cupcake Wars*, in the heat of battle, I forgot to add the pumpkin in the pumpkin cupcake challenge. The judges loved the cupcake but I was voted off for not using all the ingredients. I then became known as the "pumpkin guy"!

MAKES 12 CUPCAKES

1. To make the cupcakes, preheat the oven to 350°F. Line a 12-cup muffin tin with paper cupcake liners.

2. In a medium bowl, whisk together the flour, cinnamon, ginger, allspice, nutmeg, baking powder, baking soda, and salt. Set aside.

This is the cupcake that put us on the map.

3. In a large bowl using a hand mixer, beat together the butter and granulated sugar until light and fluffy, 3 to 4 minutes. Add the pumpkin and vanilla. Add the eggs one at a time, mixing until each addition is incorporated before adding the next. Add the flour mixture and mix until thoroughly combined.

4. Fill each cupcake liner three-quarters full with batter. Bake for 20 to 23 minutes, until a toothpick inserted into the center of a cupcake comes out clean. Let cool completely on a wire rack before frosting.

5. To make the cardamom buttercream, in a large bowl using a hand mixer, beat together the butter, vanilla, cardamom, and milk. Gradually add the confectioners' sugar and beat until thoroughly combined and smooth.

6. Transfer the frosting to a pastry bag fitted with a plain tip and pipe a swirl of frosting on top of each cupcake. Store in an airtight container in refrigerator for up to 3 days.

Big Scoops

Nutella-Wella Ice Cream   42

Pecan-Caramel Crunch Ice Cream   45

Blueberry Muffin Ice Cream   47

Cinnamon Crunch Ice Cream   50

Fudgy Chocoholic Ice Cream   52

Red Velvet Ice Cream   55

Lily's Strawberry Ice Cream   57

and

Salted Caramel Ice Cream   58

NUTELLA-WELLA
ICE CREAM

6 egg yolks

1 cup half-and-half

1½ cups Nutella, at room temperature, divided

Pinch of salt

2 cups heavy cream

My son, Jax, loves Nutella. One morning he asked if he could help make a Nutella ice cream. So we started experimenting that day and came up with this very popular ice cream.

MAKES 1 QUART

1. In a medium bowl, whisk together the egg yolks, half-and-half, 1 cup of the Nutella, and the salt. Set aside.

2. Place a few cups of ice in a large bowl. Set a medium bowl inside the larger bowl of ice. Place a fine strainer over the medium bowl and set aside.

3. In a heavy saucepan, heat the cream over medium heat until just before it comes to the boil (it will bubble along the edges). Turn off the heat. Slowly whisk the hot cream into the egg yolk mixture, a little at a time, being careful not to curdle the eggs. Once incorporated, pour the entire custard mixture back into the saucepan and cook over medium heat, stirring continuously, until it thickens slightly. The custard is ready when it coats the back of a spoon. (If you want to use a candy thermometer, you're shooting for 175°F.) Pour the custard through the strainer into the medium bowl. Add just enough water to the ice so that the cold water rises up to the level of the custard. Stir the custard occasionally until it is cool. Remove from the ice bath and cover with plastic wrap. Refrigerate for several hours.

continued on page 44

NUTELLA-WELLA ICE CREAM
CONTINUED

4. Place a 1-quart storage container in the freezer, preferably something flat so that it's easy to swirl in the remaining Nutella. Transfer the chilled custard to an ice cream maker and churn according to the manufacturer's instructions.

5. Fill the frozen container halfway with the ice cream. Drizzle ¼ cup of the Nutella all over the surface. With a fork, swirl it through the ice cream. Break up large blobs of Nutella because once frozen, they are hard to chew and make the ice cream challenging to scoop. Cover with the remaining ice cream. Swirl the remaining ¼ cup Nutella into the ice cream. Cover and freeze for a few hours or overnight. Store in an airtight container in the freezer for up 2 weeks.

PECAN-CARAMEL CRUNCH ICE CREAM

¾ cup quick-cooking oats

1 cup chopped pecans

¼ cup all-purpose flour

2¼ cups firmly packed light brown sugar, divided

4 tablespoons (½ stick) unsalted butter, melted

3 cups whole milk

1 (12-ounce) can evaporated milk

½ teaspoon salt

4 large egg yolks

4 cups heavy cream

1 (14-ounce) can sweetened condensed milk

2 tablespoons pure vanilla extract

1 (20-ounce) bottle caramel topping

Waffle cone pieces, store-bought, for garnish

The vanilla base in this recipe is very sweet and rich. The crunch comes from a combination of oats and pecans.

MAKES 1 QUART

1. Preheat the oven to 350°F.

2. In a medium bowl, stir together the oats, pecans, flour, ¼ cup of the brown sugar, and the butter. Spread the mixture in a thin layer on a rimmed baking sheet and bake for 15 minutes, until lightly brown. Let cool completely on a wire rack.

3. Transfer the oat mixture to a food processor and pulse until finely chopped; set aside.

4. In a large saucepan, stir together the remaining 2 cups brown sugar, the whole milk, the evaporated milk, and salt and bring to a simmer over low heat. Simmer, stirring often, for 1 minute. (Do not boil.)

continued

PECAN-CARAMEL CRUNCH ICE CREAM
CONTINUED

5. In a medium bowl, beat the egg yolks until thick and lemon colored. Gradually stir 1 cup of the hot brown sugar mixture into the egg yolks. Pour the egg yolk mixture back into the saucepan with the milk mixture; cook, stirring continuously, over low heat for 2 minutes, or until the mixture begins to thicken. Remove the pan from the heat; stir in the cream, condensed milk, and vanilla. Let cool to room temperature.

6. Pour the mixture into the freezer container of a 6-quart hand-turned or electric ice cream maker, and freeze according to manufacturer's instructions, 5 to 7 minutes, or until partially frozen. Layer the top of the ice cream evenly with the oat mixture and caramel topping and fold into the ice cream. Freeze according to the manufacturer's instructions, 10 to 15 minutes more, or until the mixture is completely frozen. Store in an airtight container in the freezer for up to 2 weeks.

BLUEBERRY MUFFIN ICE CREAM

2 cups whole milk, divided

1½ tablespoons cornstarch

3 tablespoons cream cheese, at room temperature

½ teaspoon sea salt

½ teaspoon ground cinnamon

1¼ cups heavy cream

⅔ cups sugar

1 tablespoon pure vanilla extract

2 tablespoons light corn syrup

2 to 3 of your favorite blueberry muffins, crumbled

This is what breakfast should taste like every morning. Sprinkle the top with a few fresh blueberries when serving.

MAKES 1 QUART

1. In a small bowl, whisk together 2 tablespoons of the milk with the cornstarch until smooth. Set aside.

2. In a large bowl, whisk together the cream cheese, salt, and cinnamon until smooth.

3. Fill another very large bowl halfway full with cold water and a few ice cubes. Set aside.

4. In a large saucepan, heat the remaining milk, heavy cream, sugar, vanilla, and corn syrup over medium heat, whisking frequently. Bring to a rolling boil, and boil for 4 minutes. Remove from the heat and very slowly whisk in the cornstarch mixture. Return to the heat and bring to a rolling boil again, this time stirring with a spatula while the mixture thickens just slightly, 1 to 2 minutes.

continued

5. Remove from the heat and very slowly pour a small amount of the milk mixture into the cream cheese mixture, whisking continuously until smooth. While whisking, gradually pour the rest of the milk mixture into the bowl. Pour the slightly cooled custard into a 1-gallon resealable freezer bag, pushing the air out and sealing it. Place the bag in the ice bath for 30 to 45 minutes, until cold, adding more ice if needed.

6. Transfer the cooled custard to an ice cream maker and churn according to the manufacturer's directions. After 20 to 22 minutes, add 2 to 3 crumbled blueberry muffins. Transfer the ice cream to a freezer-safe container, cover, and freeze for 8 hours. Store in an airtight container in the freezer for up to 2 weeks.

CINNAMON CRUNCH ICE CREAM

5 large egg yolks

2 cups heavy cream

1 cup whole milk

⅓ cup granulated sugar

⅓ cup lightly packed light brown sugar

⅛ teaspoon salt

1 teaspoon pure vanilla extract

2 teaspoons ground cinnamon

⅔ cup cinnamon chips

¼ teaspoon coconut or vegetable oil (optional)

1 cup crispy rice cereal

Cinnamon Toast Crunch is one of my favorite breakfast cereals. This recipe tastes just like it, but with the milk already added.

MAKES 1 QUART

1. In a medium bowl, whisk the egg yolks and set aside.

2. In a medium saucepan, combine the cream, milk, granulated sugar, brown sugar, and salt and bring to a simmer over medium heat. Just before the cream mixture comes to a boil, remove from the heat. Slowly pour about one-third of the hot cream mixture into the egg yolks, whisking constantly so the eggs don't curdle.

3. Return the mixture to the saucepan with the cream mixture and cook, whisking continuously, until slightly thickened. The custard is ready when it coats the back of a spoon. (If you want to use a candy thermometer, you're shooting for 175°F.)

4. Strain the custard through a fine-mesh strainer into a bowl. Whisk in the vanilla and cinnamon, then whisk occasionally as the custard cools. Once at room temperature, press a layer of cling wrap on top of the custard and refrigerate until completely chilled. (To speed up the process, you can place the bowl over an ice bath and whisk it as it cools down.)

5. While the custard chills, line a rimmed baking sheet with waxed paper. Place the cinnamon chips in a microwave-safe bowl. Microwave for 25 seconds, then stir, heating them again in short intervals, if needed, until the chips have melted. If your chips are still fairly stiff, add the coconut oil a little at a time until the melted chips are smooth and fluid. Place the crispy rice cereal in a medium bowl and pour the melted cinnamon chips over the top. Stir until the cereal is well coated. Scrape the cereal out onto the prepared baking sheet and spread it into a thin, even layer. Refrigerate until set, then use a knife or your fingers to crumble the cereal mixture into small pieces.

6. When the custard is chilled and the cinnamon crunch is ready, place a 9 by 5-inch loaf pan in the freezer. Transfer the chilled custard to an ice cream maker and churn according to the manufacturer's instructions. Stir in the cinnamon crunch. Scrape the ice cream into the chilled loaf pan and smooth it into an even layer. Cover the ice cream with plastic wrap and freeze to firm up completely. Store in an airtight container in the freezer for up to 2 weeks.

FUDGY CHOCOHOLIC ICE CREAM

7 ounces dark chocolate
(70 to 75% cacao), finely chopped

2 cups plus 2 tablespoons whole milk

⅓ cup unsweetened Dutch-process
 cocoa powder

6 large egg yolks

13 tablespoons sugar, divided

¼ cup heavy cream

This chocolate ice cream recipe gets an extra dose of richness from two different types of chocolate. The mix of dark chocolate pieces with very fine Dutch-process cocoa will delight chocolate-lovers!

MAKES 1 QUART

1. Place a few cups of ice in a large bowl. Set a second large bowl inside the larger bowl of ice and set aside.

2. Place the dark chocolate in a microwave-safe bowl and microwave in 30-second bursts, stirring after each interval, until the chocolate is completely melted and smooth. Set aside to cool slightly.

3. In a large saucepan, whisk together the milk and cocoa powder. Bring to boil over medium heat, then remove from the heat and set aside to cool slightly.

4. In a medium bowl using a hand mixer, beat the egg yolks and 7 tablespoons of the sugar on high until the mixture is pale and forms very thick ribbons when you lift the beaters out of the bowl, about 3 minutes.

continued on page 54

5. Whisking continuously, gradually add the slightly cooled milk mixture to the egg yolks until combined.

6. Return the mixture to the saucepan and whisk in the melted chocolate until blended. Return the pan to low heat and stir continuously, getting into the corners of the pan, until slightly thickened and a thermometer registers 175°F, about 5 minutes.

7. Transfer the chocolate custard to the large bowl set in the ice bath to cool. Stir until the custard is cool.

8. Meanwhile, in a small, heavy, deep saucepan, combine the remaining 6 tablespoons sugar and 2 tablespoons water and bring to a boil over medium-high heat, stirring, until the sugar dissolves.

9. Caramelize the sugar over high to medium-high heat, occasionally swirling the pan and brushing down sides with a wet pastry brush to dissolve any sugar crystals (do not stir), until a dark amber color forms, about 5 minutes. Gradually whisk in the cream.

10. Whisk the caramel into the chocolate custard. Strain through a fine-mesh sieve into a large container. Cover and refrigerate for 2 days.

11. Transfer the chilled custard to an ice cream maker and churn according to the manufacturer's instructions. Transfer to an airtight container, cover, and freeze. Store in an airtight container in the freezer for up to 2 weeks.

RED VELVET
ICE CREAM

1½ (8-ounce) packages cream cheese, at room temperature

2 cups sour cream

1 cup half-and-half

1½ cups sugar

Pinch of salt

2 cups red velvet cake crumbs (see page 11)

We decided to take our most popular cupcake and turn it into ice cream. The cream cheese ice cream is our version of frosting on a cupcake.

MAKES 1 QUART

1. Cut the cream cheese into small pieces and place in a food processor or blender. Add the sour cream, half-and-half, sugar, and salt and process until smooth. Transfer the mixture to an airtight container and refrigerate for at least 8 hours.

2. Transfer the chilled ice cream base to an ice cream maker and churn according to the manufacturer's instructions.

3. Place the cake crumbs in a large bowl. Once the ice cream has finished churning, add it to the cake crumbs and quickly fold the crumbs into the ice cream. Cover the bowl and freeze for at least a few hours to allow the ice cream to harden. Store in an airtight container in the freezer for up to 2 weeks.

This recipe is hands down my favorite ice cream flavor.

LILY'S STRAWBERRY ICE CREAM

1 (14-ounce) can sweetened condensed milk

1 (5-ounce) can evaporated milk

1½ cups whole milk

2 tablespoons sugar

1 (16-ounce) container fresh strawberries, hulled, or 1 (16-ounce) package frozen strawberries, thawed and drained

2 tablespoons fresh lemon juice

¼ teaspoon salt

This my daughter Lily's favorite ice cream. She loves picking strawberries and asked if we could make the ice cream sweet like strawberries. The great thing about this recipe is that it uses sweetened condensed milk, which makes it very rich and creamy.

MAKES 1 QUART

1. In a 2-quart pitcher or a large bowl, whisk together the condensed milk, evaporated milk, whole milk, and sugar until blended. Cover and refrigerate for 30 minutes.

2. In a blender or food processor, blend the strawberries, lemon juice, and salt until smooth. Stir into the milk mixture.

3. Transfer the ice cream base to an ice cream maker and churn according to the manufacturer's instructions.

4. Remove the container from the ice-cream maker, and place in the freezer for 15 minutes. Transfer to an airtight container; freeze until firm, about 1 to 1½ hours. Store in an airtight container in the freezer for up to 2 weeks.

SALTED CARAMEL ICE CREAM

1¼ cups sugar, divided

2¼ cups heavy cream, divided

½ teaspoon flaky sea salt

½ teaspoon pure vanilla extract

1 cup whole milk

3 large eggs

The blend of caramel and salt in this recipe will have your taste buds singing. It's even better served with a few crushed pretzels on top.

MAKES 1 QUART

1. In a skillet, heat 1 cup of the sugar over medium heat, stirring with a fork to heat the sugar evenly. Once it starts to melt, stop stirring and cook, only swirling occasionally so the sugar melts evenly to become a dark amber color.

2. Add 1¼ cups of the cream and cook, stirring, until all of the caramel has dissolved. Transfer to a bowl and stir in the salt and vanilla. Let cool to room temperature.

3. Meanwhile, in a small saucepan, combine the milk, remaining 1 cup cream, and remaining ¼ cup sugar and heat over medium heat, stirring occasionally, until the mixture just comes to a boil.

4. In a medium bowl, lightly whisk the eggs. While whisking continuously, add half the hot milk mixture to the eggs in a slow stream. Pour the mixture back into the saucepan and cook over medium heat, stirring continuously with a wooden spoon, until the custard coats the back of the spoon. (If you want to use a candy thermometer, you're shooting for 175°F.) Pour the custard through a fine-mesh sieve into a large bowl, then stir in the cooled caramel. Cover and refrigerate, stirring occasionally, until very cold, 3 to 6 hours.

5. Transfer the chilled custard to an ice cream maker and freeze according to the manufacturer's instructions. Transfer the ice cream to an airtight container, cover, and freeze to firm up. Store in an airtight container in the freezer for up to 2 weeks.

Sweet Treats

1¾ cups all-purpose flour

2 tablespoons nonfat milk powder

1½ teaspoons salt

½ teaspoon baking powder

½ teaspoon baking soda

¾ cup (1½ sticks) unsalted butter, at room temperature

1 cup granulated sugar

½ cup lightly packed brown sugar

1 large egg

1 teaspoon pure vanilla extract

⅔ cup mini semisweet chocolate chips

1½ cups mini marshmallows

3 cups cornflakes

This is no ordinary cookie; it's very unique because it has everything.

CORNFLAKE-MARSHMALLOW CHOCOLATE CHIP COOKIES

When you take a bite, you'll be rewarded with a chewy chocolate chip cookie taste filled with little tiny pockets of marshmallow and finished with a little crunch from the cornflakes. Pure magic.

MAKES 12 COOKIES

1. In a large bowl, whisk together the flour, milk powder, salt, baking powder, and baking soda. Set aside.

2. In a separate large bowl using a hand mixer, beat together the butter, granulated sugar, brown sugar, egg, and vanilla on high for 2 to 3 minutes, until creamy. Gradually add the flour mixture in two separate additions, mixing on low until the dough just comes together.

3. Add the chocolate chips and mix on low to distribute. Reserve handful of the marshmallows to decorate the cookies and add the remaining marshmallows to the dough, mixing on low until evenly distributed.

4. Carefully mix in the cornflakes by hand so they don't get too crushed. Cover the dough and refrigerate for 1 hour.

5. Preheat the oven to 350°F. Line a baking sheet with parchment paper.

6. Roll the dough into golf ball–size balls and place on prepared baking sheet, spacing them about 3 inches apart. Press a marshmallow or two on top of each cookie. Make sure they have ample room to spread out. Bake for 13 minutes, until light brown. Let cool on the baking sheet. Store in an airtight container at room temperature for up to 1 week.

cookies

1 cup quick-cooking oats

1¾ cups plus 2 tablespoons all-purpose flour

2 teaspoons unsweetened cocoa powder

1½ teaspoons cornstarch

1 teaspoon baking powder

½ teaspoon baking soda

¾ teaspoon ground cinnamon

¼ teaspoon freshly grated nutmeg

¼ teaspoon ground ginger

¾ teaspoon salt

½ cup (1 stick) unsalted butter, at room temperature

½ cup vegetable shortening

1¼ cups granulated sugar

2½ tablespoons molasses

2 large eggs

1 teaspoon pure vanilla extract

⅛ teaspoon coconut extract

OATMEAL CREAM PIE COOKIES

The marshmallow creme filling here tastes just like the Little Debbie Creme Pies. These take me back to being a kid and opening that package of delight in a school lunch.

MAKES 15 SANDWICH COOKIES

1.   To make the cookies, preheat the oven to 350°F. Line two baking sheets with parchment paper.

2.   In a food processor, pulse the oats 10 to 15 times, until they are about half their original size. Transfer to a medium bowl and add the flour, cocoa powder, cornstarch, baking powder, baking soda, cinnamon, nutmeg, ginger, and salt. Whisk to combine and set aside.

3.   In the bowl of a stand mixer fitted with the paddle attachment, whip the butter, shortening, sugar, and molasses on medium-high speed until pale and fluffy, about 2 minutes. Add the eggs one at a time, mixing well after each addition and scraping down the bowl as needed. Mix in the vanilla and coconut extract. Slowly add the flour mixture and mix until well combined.

4. Scoop out 2 tablespoon portions of the dough and roll them into balls. Place the balls on the prepared baking sheet at least 2½ inches apart (you should have 9 cookies per sheet). Bake for 10 to 12 minutes. The cookies should still be soft, not fully set—be careful not to overbake them. Let cool for 5 to 10 minutes on the baking sheet.

5. To make the marshmallow creme filling, in the bowl of a stand mixer fitted with the paddle attachment, whip together the butter and shortening on medium-high speed until pale and fluffy, 3 to 4 minutes. Add the confectioners' sugar and beat on low speed until combined. Raise the speed to medium-high and beat for 1 minute. Reduce the speed to low and mix in the marshmallow creme.

6. To assemble the cookies, spread 1½ to 2 tablespoons of the marshmallow filling over the flat bottom side of one cookie and sandwich to the bottom side of another cookie. Store the sandwich cookies in an airtight container in the refrigerator for up to 2 weeks.

marshmallow creme filling

½ cup (1 stick) unsalted butter, nearly at room temperature

¼ cup vegetable shortening

1½ cups confectioners' sugar

7 ounces marshmallow creme

CREAMY RASPBERRY ICE POPS

1½ cups skim milk, divided

1 (1-ounce) box vanilla pudding mix

1 cup fresh raspberries

2 cups reduced-fat frozen whipped topping, thawed

2 cups raspberry sherbet, softened

My mother used to make these for my brother and me every summer. We would pick fresh raspberries and then help her put it all together. The double dose of raspberry here with sherbet and fresh berries makes these totally fruity!

MAKES 10 ICE POPS

1. Pour 1 cup of the milk into a bowl and stir in the pudding mix. Beat with a hand mixer for 2 minutes until thickened.

2. In a blender, combine the remaining ½ cup milk and the raspberries and purée until smooth.

3. Pour the raspberry purée into the pudding and add the whipped topping. Stir until incorporated. Stir in the softened sherbet. You may either mix it in completely, or leave it swirled.

4. Divide this mixture evenly among ten ice pop molds or 4-ounce plastic cups. Place a wooden craft stick into each, and freeze for least 3 hours. When ready to remove the ice pops, run the mold under warm water to loosen it. Pull out the popsicle and enjoy, or store them in the molds in the freezer for up to 2 weeks.

Nothing says summer like ice pops and raspberries.

cakes

2 cups all-purpose flour

3 tablespoons unsweetened cocoa powder

½ teaspoon baking soda

½ teaspoon salt

4 tablespoons (½ stick) unsalted butter, at room temperature

¼ cup vegetable oil

1 cup granulated sugar

1 large egg

1 teaspoon pure vanilla extract

1 teaspoon distilled white vinegar

⅔ cup regular buttermilk, well-shaken

1 (1-ounce) bottle red food coloring (2 tablespoons)

creme filling

1 (8-ounce) package cream cheese, at room temperature

4 tablespoons (½ stick) unsalted butter, at room temperature

1 teaspoon fresh lemon juice

½ teaspoon pure vanilla extract

⅛ teaspoon salt

2 cups confectioners' sugar

RED VELVET WHOOPSIE PIES

This is the way to eat cupcakes. Whoopsie pies were created for Smallcakes when we had customers cutting the tops off and asking for frosting to sandwich between them. This recipe makes two small cake tops to sandwich luscious frosting between. You can really have your cake and eat it too!

MAKES 12 PIES

1. To make the cakes, preheat the oven to 350°F. Line two baking sheets with parchment paper.

2. In a large bowl, whisk together the flour, cocoa powder, baking soda, and salt. Set aside.

3. In a separate large bowl using a hand mixer, beat together the butter, oil, and granulated sugar until well combined, about 2 minutes. Beat in the egg, vanilla, and vinegar. Reduce the speed to low and in three alternating additions, add the flour mixture and buttermilk, beginning and ending with the flour and mixing well after each addition before adding the next.

4. Add the red food coloring and mix on low speed until thoroughly combined. Spoon 2-tablespoon mounds of batter, 2 inches apart, on the lined baking sheets. Bake, switching positions of the baking sheet halfway through baking, until the rounds are puffed and set, 8 to 10 minutes. Slide the parchment with the rounds onto wire racks to cool completely.

5. To make the creme filling, in a large bowl using a hand mixer, beat together the cream cheese, butter, lemon juice, vanilla, salt, and confectioners' sugar until creamy, 1 to 2 minutes. Spread about 2 tablespoons of the filling on the flat side of half the rounds; top with the remaining rounds, flat-side down, to form whoopsie pies. Store in an airtight container in the refrigerator for up to 1 week.

SPICED APPLE-PEAR PIES IN A JAR

1 cup diced peeled apples

1 cup diced peeled pears

2 tablespoons all-purpose flour

2 tablespoons light brown sugar

2 teaspoons ground cinnamon

1 teaspoon freshly grated nutmeg

Pinch of salt

1 (9-inch) prepared pie crust

2 tablespoons butter, diced

Cinnamon Crunch Ice Cream
(page 50), for serving

Mason jar desserts are a great addition to any party; they are not hard to make and look great on dessert tables. You can find the reusable 4-ounce jars at most hardware stores, and the top doubles as a cookie cutter.

MAKES EIGHT 4-OUNCE SERVINGS

1. Preheat the oven to 350°F.

2. In a large bowl, stir together the apples, pears, flour, brown sugar, cinnamon, nutmeg, and salt. Toss until the fruit is fully coated.

3. Roll out your pie crust to a ½-inch thickness. Using the top of a 4-ounce mason jar, cut out 8 circles—these will be the top crusts. Gather up the leftover dough and divide it into 8 pieces. Line eight 4-ounce mason jars with the dough, pressing it into a thin layer until the interior of the jar is completely covered.

The addition of pears here to a traditional apple pie gives it a nice fall flavor.

continued on page 72

4. Divide the fruit mixture evenly among the mason jars and top each with a few butter cubes. Then place a top crust over each jar and press it in using a fork. Make a few small slits in the top to vent while cooking. If you are feeling fancy, you also can cut each dough circle into strips and make lattice tops on the jars.

5. Place the mason jars in a baking pan with ½ inch of water in the bottom. Bake for 35 to 40 minutes, until the crust is light brown. Check the tops at about 20 minutes. You may need to cover them with a sheet of aluminum foil to prevent the crust from burning and to allow the bottom crust to finish cooking.

6. Remove from the oven and let cool completely. Serve with a scoop of Cinnamon Maple Ice Cream.

MOM'S HOLIDAY FUDGE

1 cup (2 sticks) unsalted butter,
plus more for the pan

4 ½ cups sugar

Pinch of salt

1 (14-ounce) can evaporated milk

12 ounces semisweet chocolate chips

3 (4-ounce) bars German
sweet baking chocolate

2 (7-ounce) jars marshmallow creme

2 cups chopped pecans

2 teaspoons pure vanilla extract

The one thing I looked forward to at Christmastime each year as a kid (well, besides presents) was Mom's fudge. The evaporated milk helps keep this fudge soft and chewy, and it will be welcome at every holiday gathering.

MAKES ONE 9 BY 13-INCH PAN

1. Grease a 9 by 13-inch pan with butter.

2. In a large saucepan, combine the butter, sugar, salt, and milk and bring to a boil over medium heat. Boil for 6 minutes, or until a candy thermometer reads 234°F (soft ball stage).

3. In a large bowl, stir together the chocolate chips, German chocolate, marshmallow creme, pecans, and vanilla.

4. Pour the boiling syrup over the ingredients in the bowl and stir until the chocolate is melted. Carefully pour the fudge into the prepared pan.

5. Let stand a few hours at room temperature before cutting the fudge into pieces of the desired size. Store the fudge layered between waxed paper in an airtight container in the refrigerator for up to 2 weeks.

lemon cupcakes

1¼ cups cake flour

1¼ teaspoons baking powder

½ teaspoon baking soda

½ teaspoon salt

2 large eggs

¾ cup granulated sugar

½ teaspoon pure vanilla extract

1 teaspoon pure lemon extract

1 teaspoon finely grated lemon zest

2 tablespoons fresh lemon juice

½ cup vegetable, canola,
or extra-light olive oil

½ cup sour cream

strawberry frosting

½ cup (1 stick) unsalted butter

4 ounces cream cheese

4 cups confectioners' sugar

1 teaspoon pure vanilla extract

2 to 3 tablespoons strawberry jam

1 tablespoon heavy cream or
whole milk, as needed

4 to 6 fresh strawberries, hulled
and sliced, for garnish

STRAWBERRY LEMONADE CUPCAKES IN A JAR

These mason jars look amazing with the bright colors of the layers of cake and frosting. These work well for a great spring or summer party. Add some of Lily's Strawberry Ice Cream (page 57) on the side for an added serving of strawberry goodness.

MAKES TWENTY-FOUR 4-OUNCE JARS

1. To make the lemon cupcakes, preheat the oven to 350°F. Line two 12-cup muffin tins with paper cupcake liners.

2. In a medium bowl, whisk together the flour, baking powder, baking soda, and salt. Set aside.

3. In the bowl of a stand mixer fitted with the paddle attachment, beat the eggs for 10 to 20 seconds. Add the granulated sugar and beat on medium speed for about 30 seconds more. Add the vanilla, lemon extract, lemon zest, lemon juice, and oil and beat until smooth. Add the sour cream and blend until combined. Reduce the mixer speed to low and slowly add the flour mixture. Mix just until the dry ingredients are incorporated.

4. Fill the cupcake liners about two-thirds full with the batter. Bake for 12 to 15 minutes, until a toothpick inserted into the center of a cupcake comes out clean. Let cool completely before frosting.

continued

5. To make the strawberry frosting, in a large bowl using a hand mixer, beat the butter until completely smooth. Add the cream cheese and beat until fully incorporated and very smooth.

6. With the mixer running on low speed, add the confectioners' sugar, 1 cup at a time. Add the vanilla and strawberry jam and beat until well combined. If the frosting is very thick, add a little bit of the heavy cream, then beat until light and fluffy.

7. To assemble the jars, first remove the cupcake liners from the cooled cupcakes and then slice each in half horizontally. Place the bottom half of a cupcake in each jar. Transfer the frosting to a pastry bag fitted with a plain tip and pipe a layer of frosting in each of the twenty-four 4-ounce mason jars. Then place the top of a cupcake on top of each one and finish with a layer of frosting. Garnish with fresh strawberries, as desired. Store in an airtight container in the refrigerator for up to 1 week.

METRIC CONVERSIONS AND EQUIVALENTS

Approximate Metric Equivalents

volume

¼ teaspoon	1 milliliter
½ teaspoon	2.5 milliliters
¾ teaspoon	4 milliliters
1 teaspoon	5 milliliters
1¼ teaspoon	6 milliliters
1½ teaspoon	7.5 milliliters
1¾ teaspoon	8.5 milliliters
2 teaspoons	10 milliliters
1 tablespoon (½ fluid ounce)	15 milliliters
2 tablespoons (1 fluid ounce)	30 milliliters
¼ cup	60 milliliters
⅓ cup	80 milliliters
½ cup (4 fluid ounces)	120 milliliters
⅔ cup	160 milliliters
¾ cup	180 milliliters
1 cup (8 fluid ounces)	240 milliliters
1¼ cups	300 milliliters
1½ cups (12 fluid ounces)	360 milliliters
1⅔ cups	400 milliliters
2 cups (1 pint)	460 milliliters
3 cups	700 milliliters
4 cups (1 quart)	0.95 liter
1 quart plus ¼ cup	1 liter
4 quarts (1 gallon)	3.8 liters

weight

¼ ounce	7 grams
½ ounce	14 grams
¾ ounce	21 grams
1 ounce	28 grams
1¼ ounces	35 grams
1½ ounces	42.5 grams
1⅔ ounces	45 grams
2 ounces	57 grams
3 ounces	85 grams
4 ounces (¼ pound)	113 grams
5 ounces	142 grams
6 ounces	170 grams
7 ounces	198 grams
8 ounces (½ pound)	227 grams
16 ounces (1 pound)	454 grams
35.25 ounces (2.2 pounds)	1 kilogram

length

⅛ inch	3 millimeters
¼ inch	6 millimeters
½ inch	1¼ centimeters
1 inch	2½ centimeters
2 inches	5 centimeters
2½ inches	6 centimeters
4 inches	10 centimeters
5 inches	13 centimeters
6 inches	15¼ centimeters
12 inches (1 foot)	30 centimeters

Common Ingredients and Their Approximate Equivalents

1 cup all-purpose flour = 140 grams

1 stick butter (4 ounces • ½ cup • 8 tablespoons) = 110 grams

1 cup butter (8 ounces • 2 sticks • 16 tablespoons) = 220 grams

1 cup brown sugar, firmly packed = 225 grams

1 cup granulated sugar = 200 grams

Metric Conversion Formulas

to convert	multiply
Ounces to grams	Ounces by 28.35
Pounds to kilograms	Pounds by .454
Teaspoons to milliliters	Teaspoons by 4.93
Tablespoons to milliliters	Tablespoons by 14.79
Fluid ounces to milliliters	Fluid ounces by 29.57
Cups to milliliters	Cups by 236.59
Cups to liters	Cups by .236
Pints to liters	Pints by .473
Quarts to liters	Quarts by .946
Gallons to liters	Gallons by 3.785
Inches to centimeters	Inches by 2.54

Oven Temperatures

To convert Fahrenheit to Celsius, subtract 32 from Fahrenheit, multiply the result by 5, then divide by 9.

description	fahrenheit	celsius	british gas mark
Very cool	200°	95°	0
Very cool	225°	110°	¼
Very cool	250°	120°	½
Cool	275°	135°	1
Cool	300°	150°	2
Warm	325°	165°	3
Moderate	350°	175°	4
Moderately hot	375°	190°	5
Fairly hot	400°	200°	6
Hot	425°	220°	7
Very hot	450°	230°	8
Very hot	475°	245°	9

Information compiled from a variety of sources, including *Recipes into Type* by Joan Whitman and Dolores Simon (Newton, MA: Biscuit Books, 1993); *The New Food Lover's Companion* by Sharon Tyler Herbst (Hauppauge, NY: Barron's, 2013); and *Rosemary Brown's Big Kitchen Instruction Book* (Kansas City, MO: Andrews McMeel, 1998).

INDEX

Andrews McMeel Publishing, LLC
an Andrews McMeel Universal company
1130 Walnut Street, Kansas City, Missouri 64106
www.andrewsmcmeel.com

15 16 17 18 19 TEN 10 9 8 7 6 5 4 3 2

ISBN: 978-1-4494-6809-5

Library of Congress Control Number: 2014953630

PHOTOGRAPHY: Jenny Wheat
PROP STYLIST: Anna Sabatini
EDITOR: Jean Z. Lucas
DESIGNER: Diane Marsh
ART DIRECTOR: Julie Barnes
PRODUCTION EDITOR: Maureen Sullivan
PRODUCTION MANAGER: Carol Coe
DEMAND PLANNER: Sue Eikos

ATTENTION: SCHOOLS AND BUSINESSES
Andrews McMeel books are available at quantity discounts with bulk
purchase for educational, business, or sales promotional use. For
information, please e-mail the Andrews McMeel Publishing Special Sales
Department: specialsales@amuniversal.com.